W9-CEM-896

WRITE THE POEM

imagination
genius
inspiration
clever **Creativity** inventive
vision
talent
originality

honor
debt
humility
thankful **Gratitude** grace
recognition
praise
profound

transmutation
switch
variance
season **Change** shift
revision
metamorphosis
transition

tune
choral
rhythm
popular **Music** melody
orchestra
instrumental
hymn

tour
voyage
trip
expedition **Travel** trek
touring
wandering
ramble

enchantment
flame
youth
passion **First Love** tenderness
cherishing
yearning
relish

sultry
dog days
seaside
sweat **Summer** sunshine
vacation
beach
heat

Follow us on social media!

Tag us and use #piccadillyinc in your posts
for a chance to win monthly prizes!

This edition published by Piccadilly (USA) Inc.

Piccadilly (USA) Inc.
12702 Via Cortina, Suite 203
Del Mar, CA 92014
USA

10 9 8 7 6 5 4 3 2 1

Printed in China

ISBN-13: 978-1-60863-406-4

Write a poem about

The Ocean

Word Associations

billows

deep

brine

offing

wave

flux

tide

current

Word Associations

puff
mist
billow
blanket
swarm
thunderhead
nebulous
cumulous

Write a poem about

Clouds

Write a poem about

First Love

Word Associations

tenderness
relish
flame
yearning
cherishing
passion
enchantment
youth

Word Associations

budding
flowering
vernal
seedtime
beginnings
fresh
perennial
primrose

Write a poem about

Spring

Write a poem about

A Tree

Word Associations

sapling
woods
leaves
greenery
roots
branches
timber
forest

Word Associations

roaring
raging
blustering
tempestuous
squall
blast
gale
wrath

Write a poem about

A Storm

Write a poem about

A Sunny Day

Word Associations

luminous
summery
shining
clarion
radiant
brilliant
bask
haze

Word Associations

acrimony
ire
enmity
indignation
vexation
choler
rage
malice

Write a poem about
Anger

Write a poem about

Sadness

Word Associations

heartache
bleakness
dysphoria
woe
grief
despondent
sorrow
suffering

Word Associations

glee
rapture
ecstasy
bliss
cheer
contentment
delight
elation

Write a poem about

Joy

Write a poem about

Tears

Word Associations

crying
distress
grieving
sorrow
pain
weep
wailing
whimpering

Word Associations

deluge
showers
dew
precipitation
torrent
raindrops
sprinkle
liquid sunshine

Write a poem about

Rain

Write a poem about

Illness

Word Associations

malady
breakdown
affliction
ailing
relapse
disability
convalescence
recovery

Word Associations

grin
laugh
amusement
delight
smirk
beam
dimple
lips

Write a poem about

Smiles

Write a poem about

Music

Word Associations

melody
hymn
instrumental
orchestra
popular
tune
choral
rhythm

Word Associations

trek
ramble
wandering
touring
expedition
tour
voyage
trip

Write a poem about

Travel

Write a poem about

Fame

Word Associations

renown
repute
standing
acknowledgement
reputation
popularity
regard
immoral

Word Associations

verse
rhyme
stanza
composition
muse
rhythm
lyric
epic

Write a poem about

Poetry

Write a poem about

Wishes

Word Associations

intention
aspiration
ambition
hope
longing
will
yearning
desire

Word Associations

fantasy
trance
thought
image
illusion
mental picture
fancy
vision

Write a poem about

Dreams

Write a poem about

Hopes

Word Associations

expectation
wish
aspiration
ambition
belief
optimism
faith
anticipation

Word Associations

fatal
lethal
life
paradise
passing
repose
silence
sleep

Write a poem about
Mortality

Write a poem about

Heaven

Word Associations

Kingdom
glory
eternity
bliss
beyond
afterworld
hereafter
eternal rest

Word Associations

guardian
idol
nurture
mother
father
childhood
upbringing
teacher

Write a poem about

Parents

Write a poem about

Children

Word Associations

toddler
play
offspring
kids
little
foundling
youngsters
youth

Word Associations

house
fireside
village
kitchen
hearth
cottage
apartment
tenement

Write a poem about

Home

Write a poem about

Work

Word Associations

toil
labor
wage
artisan
skill
exertion
effort
grind

Word Associations

imbibe
taste
chew
eat
digest
masticate
cuisine
diet

Write a poem about

Food

Write a poem about

Time

Word Associations

eternity

hours

period

era

clock

ticktock

infinity

moment

Word Associations

memory
distant
history
remembrance
antiquity
memoir
bygone
long ago

Write a poem about

The Past

Write a poem about

The Future

Word Associations

destiny
hope
potential
imminent
opportunity
fate
foresee
prophesy

Word Associations

knowledge
smart
learn
teach
training
enlightenment
intelligence
schooling

Write a poem about

Education

Write a poem about

A Garden

Word Associations

flower
petals
soil
roots
seed
rosebud
Eden
terrace

Word Associations

chill
freeze
glacier
crystal
winter
iceberg
frigid
frozen

Write a poem about

Ice

Write a poem about

Science Fiction

Word Associations

space
alien
explore
abduction
invasion
future
humanoid
galaxy

Word Associations

president
activist
revolutionary
captain
author
conqueror
hero
leader

Write a poem about

A Historical Figure

Write a poem about

Responsibility

Word Associations

cross
burden
leadership
obligation
safeguard
onus
charge
bond

Word Associations

candor
purity
reality
fact
certainty
genuine
honesty
authentic

Write a poem about
Truth

Write a poem about
Dedication

Word Associations

devotion
allegiance
commit
piety
constancy
zeal
loyalty
fervor

Word Associations

adoration
affection
yearning
flame
emotion
ardor
fondness
rapture

Write a poem about

Love

Write a poem about

Deceit

Word Associations

trickery
duplicity
lies
guile
two-faced
imposter
pretense
fraud

Word Associations

bustle
din
clamor
tumult
uproar
thunder
crescendo
cacophony

Write a poem about

Noise

Write a poem about
Loneliness

Word Associations

isolation
empty
quiet
monotony
ache
silence
longing
seclusion

Word Associations

jittery
dread
uneasy
fretful
disquietude
distress
restless
apprehension

Write a poem about

Anxiety

Write a poem about

An Animal

Word Associations

fur
tail
beast
untamed
wild
creature
mammal
feral

Word Associations

companion
dog
cat
turtle
rabbit
snake
company
parrot

Write a poem about

A Pet

Write a poem about

Snow

Word Associations

white
drifts
hush
chill
flurry
blizzard
flake
frost

Word Associations

flow
course
unstoppable
rushing
waterway
wade
bridge
rapids

Write a poem about

A River

Write a poem about

Mountains

Word Associations

peak
summit
climb
valley
slope
ascent
crag
precipice

Word Associations

friend or foe
sojourner
mysterious
guest
newcomer
migrant
visitor
acquaintance

Write a poem about

A Stranger

Write a poem about

War

Word Associations

combat
hostility
strife
bloodshed
allies
enemy
army
conflict

Word Associations

courage
sacrifice
unflinching
strength
valiant
gallant
bold
daring

Write a poem about

Heroism

Write a poem about

Cowardice

Word Associations

spineless
weak
timid
afraid
abject
pathetic
wimp
deserter

Word Associations

comradeship
fraternity
loyal
steadfast
solidarity
partner
unity
fellowship

Write a poem about

Brotherhood

Write a poem about

A Work of Art

Word Associations

portrait
brushstrokes
texture
color
craft
landscape
shade
light

Word Associations

stars
blackness
moonlight
midnight
pitch
constellations
glimmer
wakeful

Write a poem about

The Night Sky

Write a poem about

The Moon

Word Associations

crescent
sphere
orb
silver
tide
wane
lunar
Apollo

Word Associations

golden
effulgence
solstice
radiance
heat
dappled
shadow
zenith

Write a poem about

The Sun

Write a poem about

Imperfection

Word Associations

flaw
uniqueness
foible
blemish
shortcoming
nature
defect
marred

Word Associations

luck
fortune
random
fate
remote
providence
gamble
destiny

Write a poem about

Chance

Write a poem about

Serendipity

Word Associations

karma
kismet
circumstance
divine
fluke
break
happenstance
unexpected

Word Associations

flawless
supreme
paragon
diamond
pure
ideal
sublime
unattainable

Write a poem about

Perfection

Write a poem about

A Window

Word Associations

sill
pane
view
light
panorama
curtain
shutter
glass

Word Associations

shift
transition
metamorphosis
revision
season
switch
transmutation
variance

Write a poem about

Change

Write a poem about

Kisses

Word Associations

lips

cheek

warm

wet

clasp

passion

caress

embrace

Word Associations

demon
wicked
malignity
villain
harm
corrupt
nefarious
vile

Write a poem about

Evil

Write a poem about

Temptation

Word Associations

covet
allure
bait
enticing
tantalize
draw
seduction
irresistible

Word Associations

right
code
moral
truth
fair
redress
recompense
rule

Write a poem about

Justice

Write a poem about

Inequality

Word Associations

unfair
injustice
racism
difference
bias
disparity
privilege
misfortune

Word Associations

education
philosophy
light
scholarship
expertise
theory
wisdom
judgement

Write a poem about

Knowledge

Write a poem about

Freedom

Word Associations

independence
autonomy
opportunity
liberation
range
ability
laissez faire
indulgence

Word Associations

cascade
power
possibility
rapids
spray
foam
roaring
pool

Write a poem about

A Waterfall

Write a poem about

Creativity

Word Associations

inventive

originality

talent

vision

clever

imagination

genius

inspiration

Word Associations

grace
profound
praise
recognition
thankful
honor
debt
humility

Write a poem about

Gratitude

Write a poem about

Faith

Word Associations

adoration

certainty

trust

fealty

belief

conviction

confidence

dogma

Word Associations

harm
brutality
aggression
pain
injury
attack
assault
tumult

Write a poem about

Violence

Write a poem about

Tragedy

Word Associations

doom
adversity
death
wreck
catastrophe
affliction
misfortune
curse

Word Associations

sunshine
heat
beach
vacation
sweat
sultry
dog days
seaside

Write a poem about

Summer

Write a poem about

Winter

Word Associations

snow
chill
solstice
igloo
yule
fireside
evergreen
arctic

Word Associations

autumn
orange
foliage
harvest
leaves
branches
cornucopia
death

Write a poem about

Fall

Write a poem about

Ecology

Word Associations

preservation
conservation
ecosystem
environment
science
nature
Earth
planet

Word Associations

God
otherworldly
worship
creed
principle
faith
teachings
passion

Write a poem about

Spirituality

Write a poem about
Prayer

Word Associations

invocation
entreat
appeal
humble
thanks
psalm
deliverance
blessing

Word Associations

comfort
tenderness
sharing
closeness
reassurance
glow
affection
radiate

Write a poem about

Warmth

Write a poem about

Scared

Word Associations

aghast
stricken
fearful
danger
risk
unsure
panic
afraid

Word Associations

values
custom
heritage
legend
fable
culture
folklore
convention

Write a poem about

Tradition

Write a poem about

A Glance

Word Associations

brief
impression
fleeting
shy
blink
eye contact
peek
flash

Word
Associations

bereaved
loss
sorrow
tears
lament
anguish
heartache
woe

Write a poem about
Grief

Write a poem about

Beauty

Word Associations

behold
brilliance
lovely
pathos
muse
elegance
striking
exquisite

Word Associations

wholehearted
innocence
artless
honesty
guileless
simple
genuine
plain

Write a poem about

Sincerity

Write a poem about

Captivity

Word Associations

caged
imprisonment
bondage
unfree
ransom
prison
hostage
bound

Word Associations

awe
marvel
curiosity
jolt
reverence
admiration
perplexity
fascination

Write a poem about

Wonder

Write a poem about

Affection

Word Associations

crush
itch
amore
devotion
caring
warmth
tingle
tender

Word Associations

joy
euphoria
paradise
rapture
glory
nirvana
ecstasy
completeness

Write a poem about

Bliss

Write a poem about

Broken Heart

Word Associations

stricken
heartsick
pain
doleful
betrayal
vulnerable
crushed
regret

Word Associations

stroll
fresh air
pulse
footsteps
path
promenade
breeze
wander

Write a poem about

A Walk

Write a poem about

Intelligence

Word Associations

insight
literate
shrewd
brains
discern
mind
brilliance
sense

Word Associations

freedom
soar
glide
voyage
wing
perspective
omen
breeze

Write a poem about

A Bird in Flight

Write a poem about

Flavors

Word Associations

taste
sweet
zest
savor
essence
spicy
tang
relish

Word Associations

lion
dignity
pomp
ostentation
arrogance
boast
confidence
ego

Write a poem about

Pride

Write a poem about

Weakness

Word Associations

debility
frailty
lack
folly
vice
shortcoming
feeble
vulnerability

Word Associations

destitute
waste
grief
cost
lacking
need
mourning
defeat

Write a poem about

Loss

Write a poem about

Health

Word Associations

fortitude
fettle
form
tone
vigor
potency
robust
hardy

Word Associations

esteem
brashness
assurance
morale
poise
tenacity
conviction
dignity

Write a poem about
Confidence

Write a poem about

Marriage

Word Associations

couple
alliance
love
wedlock
matrimony
mate
courtship
pledge

Word Associations

salvation
care
arms
defense
immunity
pledge
refuge
precaution

Write a poem about

Security

Write a poem about

Possibilities

Word Associations

potential
limitless
foresight
promise
action
hazard
plausible
shot

Word Associations

paragon
merit
ethical
righteous
purity
charity
worthy
upright

Write a poem about

Virtue

Write a poem about

Shock

Word Associations

crash
spark
wreck
stupor
trauma
jolt
disbelief
paralysis

Word Associations

experience
adult
sophistication
wisdom
prime
ripe
advanced
apt

Write a poem about

Maturity

Write a poem about

Treasure

Word Associations

trove
precious
rare
wealth
value
abundance
fortune
cache

Word Associations

stock
sure
credence
conviction
loyal
integrity
charge
steadfast

Write a poem about
Trust

Write a poem about

Compassion

Word Associations

benevolence
meek
tenderness
empathy
heart
clemency
mercy
softness

Word Associations

cosmos
creation
infinite
totality
relativity
immense
vast
space

Write a poem about

The Universe

Write a poem about

A Fragrance

Word Associations

bouquet
balm
aroma
savory
musk
honeysuckle
intoxicate
subtle

Word Associations

horizon
scope
dreams
visions
prospect
seize
carpe diem
luck

Write a poem about
Opportunities

Write a poem about

Meditation

Word Associations

rumination
reflection
peace
introspection
tranquil
rapt
Zen
ponder

Word Associations

parity
tolerance
balance
acceptance
fair
level
right
brotherhood

Write a poem about

Equality

Write a poem about

Independence

Word Associations

freedom
sovereign
self-reliance
autonomy
strength
confidence
assuredness
determination

Word Associations

incorrupt
honorable
constant
solid
trusty
staunch
decency
upright

Write a poem about

Reliability

Write a poem about

Challenges

Word Associations

odds
trials
dare
gauntlet
moxie
overcome
persevere
obstacle

Word Associations

stoic
serene
calm
peace
composure
humility
gentleness
placid

Write a poem about

Patience

Write a poem about

Perspective

Word Associations

viewpoint

context

scene

vista

shift

frame

broad

angle

Word Associations

passage
jaunt
journey
crossing
discovery
vessel
explore
search

Write a poem about

A Voyage

Write a poem about

Searching

Word Associations

hidden
quest
hunt
trace
rove
scour
pursue
comb

Word Associations

occasion
flash
instant
present
pause
savor
twinkling
linger

Write a poem about

Moments

Write a poem about

Frustration

Word Associations

vexation
hindrance
chagrin
failure
obstruction
foiled
bitter
setback

Word Associations

govern
dominion
restraint
clout
authority
direct
sway
monitor

Write a poem about

Control

Write a poem about

Expectations

Word Associations

promise
notion
supposition
design
motive
prospects
hope
potential

Word Associations

oneness
harmony
peace
solidarity
coherence
unanimity
collective
global

Write a poem about

Unity

Write a poem about

Blessings

Word Associations

gifts
grace
thanks
benediction
luck
boon
bestow
bounty

Word Associations

mores
scruples
ethics
standards
conscience
ideals
code
tenet

Write a poem about

Values

Write a poem about

Laughter

Word Associations

joy
belly
medicine
shriek
howl
merriment
rejoice
burst

Word Associations

hush
lull
peace
calm
quietude
stillness
whisper
profound

Write a poem about

Silence

Write a poem about

Insecurity

Word Associations

doubt
hesitancy
uncertainty
struggle
fear
exposed
misgiving
caution

Word Associations

alone
isolation
seclusion
recluse
introvert
private
remote
hermit

Write a poem about

Solitude

Write a poem about

Achievement

Word Associations

award
brass ring
accomplishment
success
posterity
crowning
victory
triumph

Word Associations

infinity
everlasting
perpetual
endless
future
immortality
eon
lasting

Write a poem about
Eternity

Write a poem about

Romance

Word Associations

thrill

amour

affair

flirtation

entangle

intimacy

passion

desire

Word Associations

enterprise
exploit
undertaking
escapade
climb
dare
gamble
voyage

Write a poem about

Adventure

Write a poem about

Angels

Word Associations

guardian
ascend
ethereal
heavenly
spirit
cherub
seraph
being

Word Associations

gratitude
tribute
thankful
salute
favor
regard
esteem
veneration

Write a poem about

Appreciation

Write a poem about

Carpe Diem

Word Associations

live
pluck
seize
dare
boldness
endeavor
audacity
nerve

Word Associations

reputation
attitude
badge
constitution
cast
tone
nature
temperament

Write a poem about

Character

Write a poem about

Colors

Word Associations

pigment
shade
tincture
complexion
scarlet
cobalt
brilliance
vermillion

Word Associations

obscure
bewilderment
turmoil
fluster
tangle
leather
turbulence
shaken

Write a poem about

Confusion

Write a poem about

Conflict

Word Associations

fray
breach
clash
rival
contest
embroil
protagonist
strife

Word Associations

prowess
spunk
intrepidity
fortitude
lion-hearted
dauntless
guts
pluck

Write a poem about

Courage

Write a poem about

Creation

Word Associations

spark
existence
genesis
animate
formation
nativity
origin
foundation

Word Associations

piety
loyalty
fidelity
earnest
sanctity
fealty
deference
service

Write a poem about

Devotion

Write a poem about

Family

Word Associations

kin
lineage
clan
tribe
blood
kindred
relationships
generation

Word Associations

clemency
compassion
mercy
absolution
lenience
charity
grace
repent

Write a poem about

Forgiveness

Write a poem about

Friendship

Word Associations

pact
brotherhood
sisterhood
league
alliance
bond
rapport
camaraderie

Word
Associations

surge
prosper
flowering
sprout
swell
unfold
boost
bud

Write a poem about

Growth

Write a poem about

Hate

Word Associations

ire

venom

spite

scorn

malevolence

aversion

bile

wrath

Word Associations

yesterday
past
antiquity
bygone
ancient
annals
chronicle
story

Write a poem about

History

Write a poem about

Humanity

Word Associations

people
mankind
good will
fellowship
civility
uprightness
forbearance
compassion

Word Associations

reserve
bashfulness
docile
meek
fawn
modesty
contrition
gentle

Write a poem about

Humility

Write a poem about

Imagination

Word Associations

vivid
invention
fantastic
stimulating
vision
enterprise
originality
artistry

Word Associations

virtue
clean
lamb
impeccable
artless
modesty
decency
temperance

Write a poem about

Innocence

Write a poem about

Inspiration

Word Associations

whimsy
insight
elation
fervor
delight
talent
fancy
revelation

Word Associations

pilgrimage
sojourn
roam
traverse
odyssey
expedition
circumnavigation
wander

Write a poem about

A Journey

Write a poem about

Judgement

Word Associations

acumen
savvy
reason
intuition
sense
perception
prudence
wisdom

Word Associations

craving
entreaty
throb
lovesick
thirst
pining
hope
languish

Write a poem about

Longing

Write a poem about

Moving On

Word Associations

hasten
momentum
go forth
launch
progress
proceed
continue
push

Word Associations

conundrum
pickle
quandary
crux
enigma
puzzlement
charade
baffle

Write a poem about

A Mystery

Write a poem about

Paradise

Word Associations

eden
Elysium
heaven
bliss
delight
utopia
transport
nirvana

Word Associations

ardor
fervor
intensity
heat
zest
lust
desire
zeal

Write a poem about

Passion

Write a poem about

Peace

Word Associations

order
truce
unity
amity
quiet
harmony
tranquility
joy

Word Associations

dream
doze
Morpheus
repose
torpor
trance
slumber
somnolence

Write a poem about

Sleep

Write a poem about

Sorrow

Word Associations

pang
mourning
misery
agony
bereavement
melancholy
woe
suffering

Word Associations

partner
lover
spouse
kindred
confidante
companion
true love
sweetheart

Write a poem about

Soul Mate

Write a poem about

Strength

Word Associations

vitality
fortitude
health
power
muscle
sinew
pith
potency

Word Associations

eventide
gloaming
nightfall
dusk
orange
gold
decline
twilight

Write a poem about

A Sunset

Write a poem about

Visions

Word Associations

perception
glimpse
insight
acumen
brilliance
fancies
musings
imagination

Word Associations

sleepless
moonless
darkness
wakeful
vigil
dim
shadow
black

Write a poem about

Nighttime

Write a poem about

Growing Older

Word Associations

golden years
mature
dotage
decline
elder
venerable
evolved
perfected

Word Associations

marriage
path
challenge
alternative
dilemma
passion vs. logic
popular
ballot

Write a poem about

A Choice

Write a poem about

Jealousy

Word Associations

rivalry

envy

antagonism

animosity

spite

grudge

covetous

strife

Word Associations

dread
tremor
paralyzed
foreboding
nightmare
creeps
jitters
angst

Write a poem about

Fear

Write a poem about

A Breath

Word Associations

inspire
expand
renewal
energize
gasp
wind
freshen
depth

Word Associations

duplicity
perfidy
Judas
Brutus
trickster
double
heartbreak
treason

Write a poem about

Betrayal

Write a poem about

A Shadow

Word Associations

two-faced
dark side
lightless
mimic
obfuscate
blacken
obscure
extinguish

Word Associations

trend
media
opinion
populism
fashion
responsibility
outcast
progress

Write a poem about

Society

Write a poem about

Seeds

Word Associations

beginnings
ideas
kernel
core
concept
embryo
germ
stem

Word Associations

oblivion
disremember
consign
escape
pass
omit
scorn
clean slate

Write a poem about

Forgetting

Write a poem about

Luck

Word Associations

stroke
profit
win
windfall
break
avail
odds
fortune

Word Associations

penitence
self-reproach
repine
bitterness
lament
bemoan
rue
defeat

Write a poem about

Regret

Write a poem about

Confessions

Word Associations

misdeeds
mistake
absolution
regrets
contrition
guilt
sacrament
forgiveness

Word Associations

matriarch
origins
childhood
warm
womb
complex
goddess
caregiver

Write a poem about

Mother

Write a poem about

Insanity

Word Associations

delirium
lunacy
mania
irrational
incoherent
delusion
neurosis
folly

Word Associations

cryptic
dark
hush
private
clouded
mist
regret
buried

Write a poem about

A Secret

Write a poem about

A Surprise

Word Associations

sudden
exclaim
unexpected
epiphany
godsend
ambush
astound
baffle

Word Associations

bind
choice
boxed in
impasse
scrape
plight
mess
quagmire

Write a poem about

Dilemma

Write a poem about

A Voice

Word Associations

murmur
whisper
holler
soft
husky
sultry
conscience
instinct

Word Associations

support
cooperation
ration
teamwork
collaboration
sacrifice
charity
generosity

Write a poem about
Sharing